WONDERFUL FAIRY TALES

GRAYSCALE COLORING BOOK FOR ADULTS

Featuring artwork by Maciej Sojka

Majestic **COLORING**

ISBN: 978-1533146632

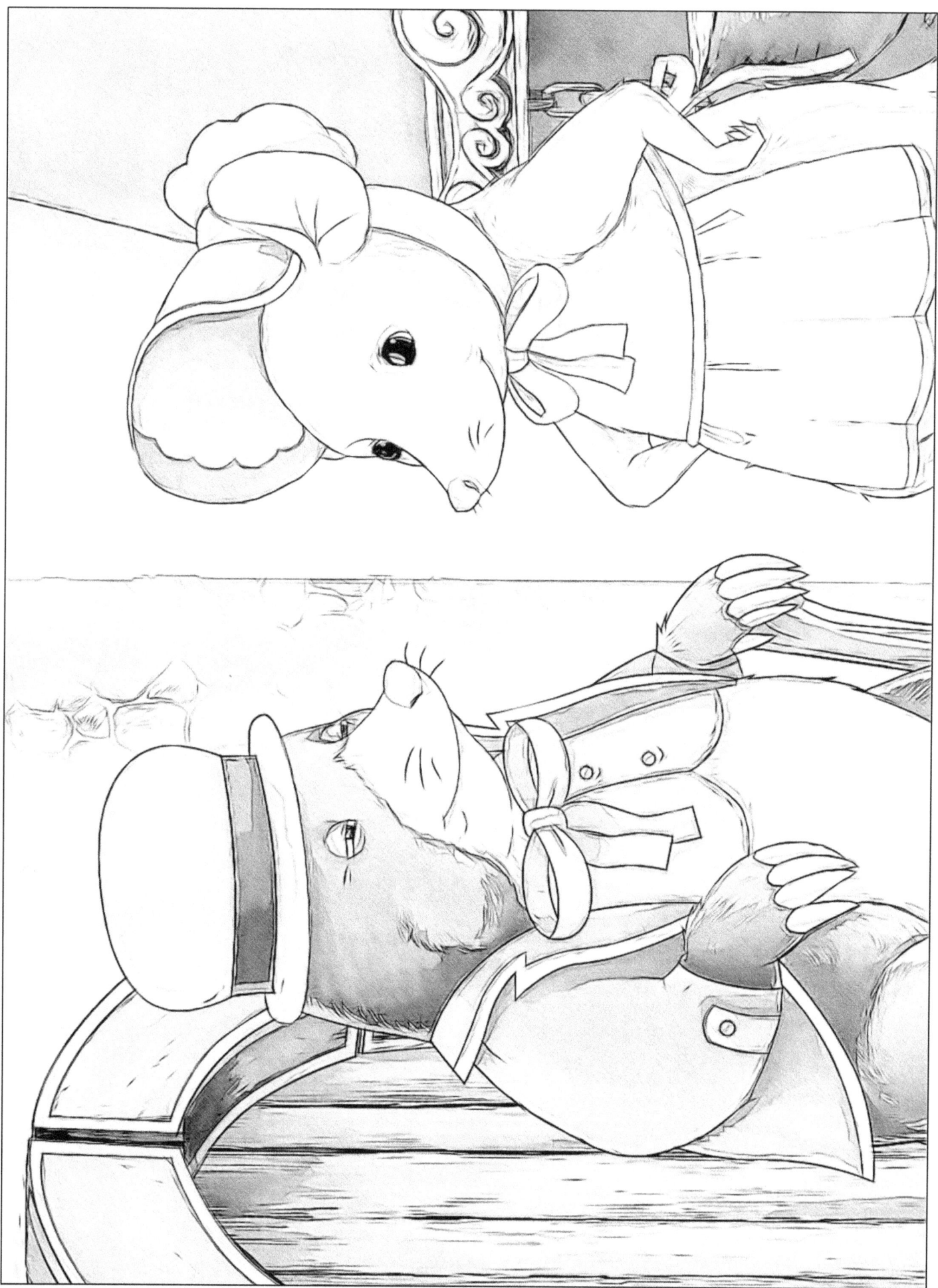

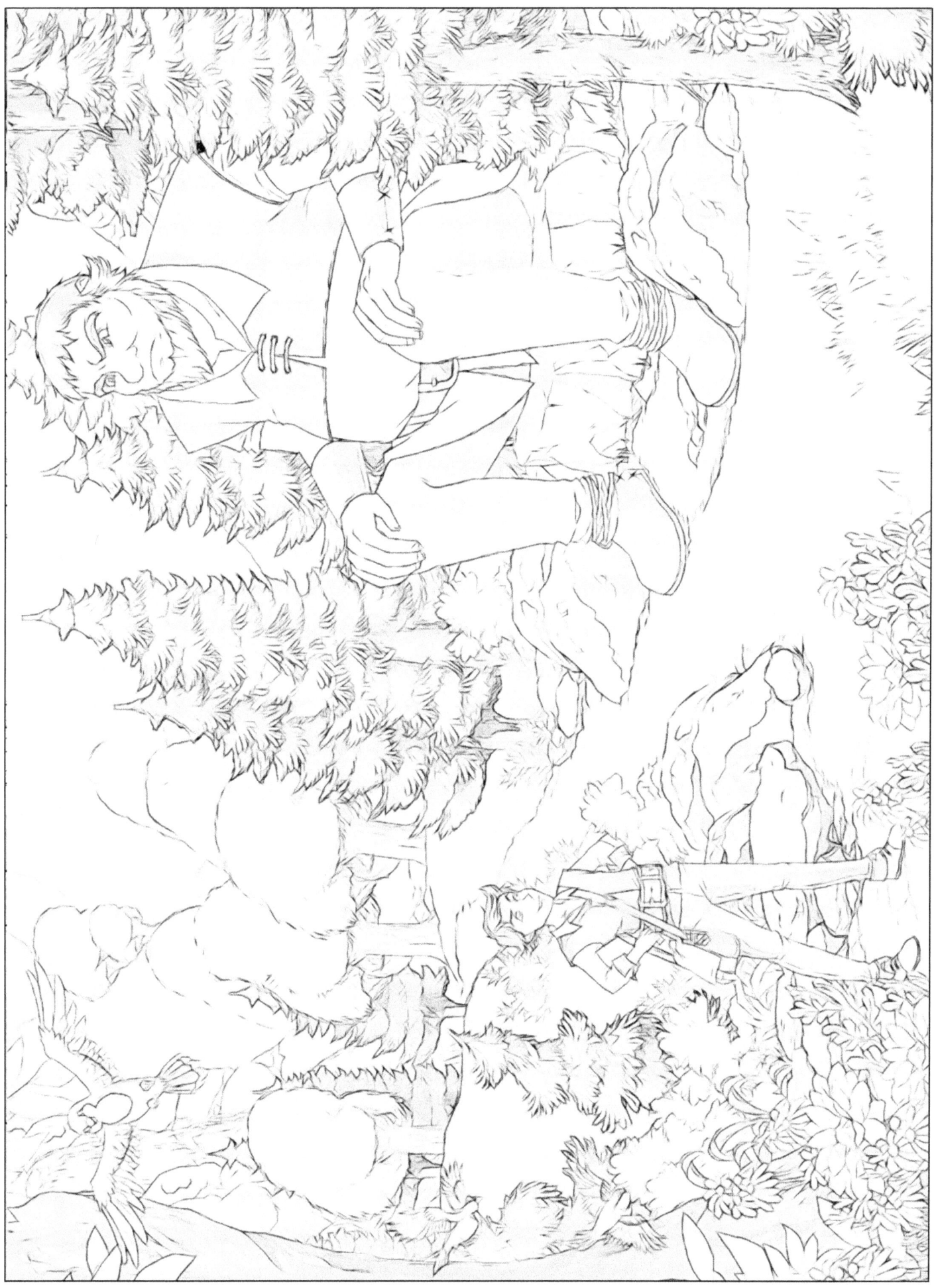

FREE DOWNLOAD

12 FUN DESIGNS FOR YOUR COLORING ENJOYMENT!

This 'n That Coloring Book for Grown-Ups is bundled up in one convenient PDF file to download and print at your leisure.

Sign up for our Majestic Coloring mailing list and get a free copy of **This 'n That Coloring Book for Grown-Ups**.

Click here to get started
http://majesticcoloring.com/thisnthat-free

www.ingramcontent.com/pod-product-compliance
Lightning Source LLC
Chambersburg PA
CBHW080703190526
45169CB00006B/2225